"When it comes to money there's facts (truth [...] tions). So often it's easy to focus on one and t[...]g talking about the subject of saving money. Kim does an incredible job getting to the heart of both in this book."

Caleb Guilliams
BetterWealth.com

"Prosperity Economics pioneer Kim Butler continues her crusade of Busting The Lies Of The Financial World! Her latest book, *Busting The Budgeting Lies,* is yet another financial game-changer that catapults the action of SAVING into the driver's seat of your financial journey, while confidently kicking the well-intended, yet ineffective ideal of budgeting to the curb.

With her ever-insightful wisdom, Kim will propel you away from the scarcity mindset of 'saving for a rainy day' and empower you to embrace the prosperity mindset of 'saving for your next sunny season.' This book delivers a transformative approach to your financial life. Don't take my word for it. Buy this book and put its insights into action and you too will transform your financial life!"

Anthony D'Angelo
Collegiate-Empowerment.org

"Wow—this book is well-written. So crisp, in a way that ChatGPT can't mimic quite yet."

Dennis Yu
BlitzMetrics.com

"Kim Butler is a pure visionary changing the world. In this, her tenth book, she showcases why budgets are like diets—they don't work and no one likes them—and reveals the keys to how wealthy families flourish with simple, easy-to-use tips. This is a must-read for anyone looking to save money, but more importantly to live a productive, cash-flow-filled life!"

Justin Breen
BrEpicLLC.com

"You can't 'homework' money, nor can you practice budgeting, so what can you do? Kim spells it out in this book and uses DinnerTable with her clients nationwide."

Scott Donnell
DinnerTable.com

"*Busting the Budgeting Lies* makes freeing oneself from typical budgeting straightforward and achievable. This guide is a lifesaver for those confined by old financial methods, offering practical steps towards a more prosperous financial future."

John Bowen
CEGworldwide.com

Busting *the* BUDGETING Lies

Lies

*Spending Plans Don't Work
—What to Do Instead*

KIM D. H. BUTLER

with E.P. Hagenlocher

Thank you for purchasing this book and supporting the work of the not-for-profit Prosperity Economics Movement, which is creating meaningful alternatives to the myths, costs, guesswork, and risks of "typical" financial planning. As a token of our appreciation, we have a gift: *How to Spend Your Principle, Save a Fortune on Taxes, Increase Your Cash Flow... and Never Run Out of Money!*

ProsperityEconomics.org/permission

Contents

PREFACE

Kids have a spot in my heart (don't they in almost everyone's?), and I am hoping this book enables a few to do a better job of picking their path after high school. Parents have earned a more efficient approach to handling the costs of supporting their children through that path, whether it be college or something else even better for their young adult. I have been honored to work with Elizabeth to write this book for both parties in hopes of creating a more sound financial future for both. If you take the typical cost of a mid-level college education and add in the opportunity cost of what that money could have done for either generation over time, it is shocking how much money it is. Please let us help you make the best with that money.

Kim Butler
Mt. Enterprise, Texas
January 2024

FOREWORD

BUDGETING SUCKS. That's why hardly anyone does it.

Budgeting implies restraint and sacrifice, rather than abundance. Thinking from a budgeting mindset lowers people's standard of living, as well as their quality of life.

Budgeting is about not creating experiences, of not taking trips, and not making memories. It's all about scrimping in the name of saving in the hope of future wealth.

Budgeting has come to mean:

We can't arrange that trip to Disneyland with the family.

We can't do date night.

I have to fire my fitness trainer who's getting me great results because he's too expensive.

In contrast, Value-Based Spending is not budgeting. It's prioritizing to get the most out of your spending.

With Value-Based Spending, you don't track your expenses down to the last penny. You don't keep receipts.

You're simply aware of how much money is flowing through your hands at any given time, by automating how you save and manage money.

Value-Based spending means understanding the difference between price, cost, and value, and spending consciously based on what we value most.

Value is perspective, so when it comes to Value-Based Spending it's our own perspective that matters.

Think of it as the difference between being cheap and being frugal. As Ramit Sethi writes in *I Will Teach You to Be Rich*, "Cheap people focus mainly on the cost of an item, while frugal people care about its value."

When you only plan for later, you neglect life itself. Budgeting destroys dreams.

When people play not to lose, it is a game of being cheap enough now, to be wealthy later. You can't scrimp your way to happiness.

The whole philosophy behind *The Millionaire Next Door* is this: If you never spend any money and you live cheaply enough, you too can become a broke millionaire.

But being a cheapskate isn't fun. What good is planning for a future when you let your actual present slip away?

You can reach economic independence and love life at the same time. It's a matter of the right methodology and mindset.

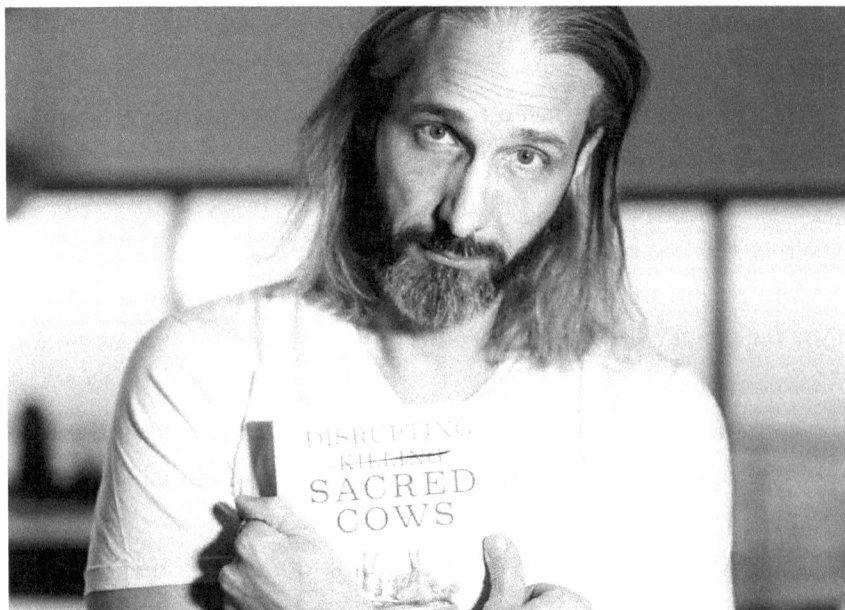

Price, Cost, and Value

There are three measures of worth for every purchase:

Price. The amount you pay for a good or service.

Cost. The economics of a deal. Cost might be measured in terms of your effort, time, lost opportunity, or degree of risk necessary to achieve a goal.

Value. The importance you place on a good or service. Your values represent your priorities and standards. Value takes into consideration such things as the type of expense, how you feel about it at the time, and if the purchase improves you as your greatest asset.

Some people think it's a waste of money to buy designer brands. Others think it's a waste of money to buy a TV sports package or season tickets for your favorite team. Others think it's a waste of money to take a European vacation.

Many personal finance gurus would say all of the above are a waste of money if you haven't saved enough for retirement yet.

Who's right? Are these purchases "worth" it?

The answer is that it depends completely on you. Price alone can't determine what something is worth. You must also consider its value—and value is perceived differently by everyone.

So if you value a Rolex watch more than you value $7,500, then anyone who tells you it's a waste of money is simply wrong.

When you follow Value-Based Spending, it's perfectly fine to live wealthy today and buy what you value. Especially if it gives you peace of mind and abundant thoughts.

When you consider the three measures of worth—price, cost, and value—deciding what to spend your money on becomes much more clear.

"Money is multiplied in practical value depending
on the number of W's you control in your life: what you do,
when you do it, where you do it, and with whom you do it."
—*Tim Ferriss*

For example, if you have the chance to buy a computer at a low cost, do you take it? You have to consider the real cost and what you value. A cheap computer may mean a slow computer, and that costs you time.

If your time is one of your most valuable assets, then pull the trigger and spend the extra money.

Some things are low price, but high cost. If you skimp on equipment trying to save a few dollars, but it doesn't get the job done right and you have to do it over, the cost can be incredibly high.

Or prices are high, but the cost is even higher, like if you prepay for a multi-year gym membership that you never use.

Some people may tell you that it makes economic sense to hire someone to mow your lawn. That may be true from a price and cost perspective.

But what if you get pleasure out of mowing your lawn? What if it helps you clear your head to make space for new ideas or simply to relax?

Then the answer is clear—you get more value out of mowing your own lawn than paying someone else to do it.

Don't let people dictate to you what's a waste of money and what's a good deal. It's completely subjective.

Follow Value-Based Spending, which doesn't constrict or constrain you, and determine the price, cost and value to make your decision.

If it adds value to your life, and contributes to your clarity, peace of mind and thinking abundantly, then it's worth it to you.

And if you value yourself—as you should—then every month, you pay a percentage of your income to yourself first, before paying for anything else.

This helps you to both expand your abundance mindset and build wealth.

Garrett Gunderson
Salt Lake City, Utah
January 2024

"Wealth is the ability to fully experience life."
—Henry David Thoreau

INTRODUCTION

BUDGETS ARE LIKE DIETS.

Just like diets restrict foods, budgets restrict spending. And while many people believe both budgets and diets to be effective, most people fail at them in the long term. The reason so many people fail, though, is because restriction is the wrong mindset to have if you want to achieve positive results (and feel good at the end of it).

Restriction is rooted in Scarcity Thinking. In finance, Scarcity Thinking is the devil on your shoulder telling you there's not enough to go around. Not enough money, time, resources—you name it! When you view the world this way, things get scary fast, and what happens when you're fearful? Your fight or flight response kicks in, and instincts compel you to make decisions that may not always be in your best interest.

That being said, budgets and diets alike have a lot of emotion tied up into them, and it's a topic that must be tread with care. We're not just here to trample on your idea of what's right when it comes to your money. Instead, we're going to address some of the myths we hear so commonly about budgeting and finance and give you our take—the Prosperity Economics way.

We won't just shatter your worldview and leave you hanging. In the pages of this book, we want to inspire you to think bigger and take a more Prosperity-based approach to your financial concerns. So rest assured, we'll give you some tools to get you headed in the right direction.

Just remember—there's no quick fix, only habits that move you closer towards your objectives one baby step at a time.

PART I: THE MYTHS

Myth #1: Budgeting Works

"So, if all you think about is budgeting,
every financial issue is a spending problem."
—*Matt J. Goran, Ph.D., from "Is Budgeting Overrated?"*

Let's get right into it: Budgeting doesn't work. You may find that shocking, coming from a financial professional, and yet I'd stand by it over and over again. *Budgeting doesn't work.*

The action of budgeting, as defined by *Webster's Dictionary*, is "to create a plan for the coordination of resources and expenditures." On paper, this sounds like the obvious solution to so many challenges that people face today. It even seems like it can work, if only you can create the right budget. And yet, in my own 30+ years of helping people with their money, I've yet to see a budget work.

Remember how I said that budgets are like diets? Nobody likes them! And when you put theory into practice, most people find that budgeting isn't enjoyable. And while adulthood means sometimes doing things you don't enjoy, that's just not how humans are wired to think. So budgeting may work for a few months, with assistance from a spreadsheet or an app, until suddenly things drop off.

This happens because what's in a budgeting app or on a spreadsheet has nothing to do with your daily life. Sure, they may be "your numbers." Yet how well do those numbers translate to the actual choices you have to make in real life?

Here are the issues:

Spending is WAY too easy when you've got a smartphone in your hand. Everything is at the click of a button, and you're constantly being targeted by ads that know exactly what you like. Ten bucks here and 30 bucks there might not seem like they'll throw off your budget too much, yet you'd be surprised.

There are too many surprises in life that immediately make your numbers inaccurate. Have you ever created the "perfect" budget, only to realize your car needs an oil change, or you didn't account for that wedding you're going to? If you've got the money, you just pay from your checking rather than pull from your savings. And while your budget might seem safe, what are you sacrificing? Your savings account? How well is that going to go for you when you have a pricier emergency?

Humans are driven by endorphins, habits, emotions, and external stimuli that throw off any financial work done on a spreadsheet or in a budgeting app. Budgets simply do not play nice in that arena.

Picture yourself, at night, on the couch or at a desk with a yellow pad or an Excel spreadsheet, doing the math to "coordinate resources and expenditures." Sometimes the result is in the black (you have enough money), and other times it's red (you don't have enough money). With this information, you try to create something "manageable," if you can, and then consider the task complete.

Then, the very next day, you're out running errands when you run into a friend. Maybe you feel compelled to go get lunch (you didn't budget for eating out), and while you're talking they mention the shiny new thing they just bought. The moment you see it, it's all you can think about, and you end up buying one too.

You see, cash flow issues don't go away, they just get bigger zeroes on them.

The problem is that despite little systematic evidence that budgeting actually helps people achieve their long-term financial goals, professionals still recommend it constantly. Of course, it may help people in the short term to pay down debt and recognize that there is a larger issue at hand, yet budgeting the way we know it is just not sustainable. Nor should you have to restrict your lifestyle so much that there's no room for the occasional treat.

So why do people keep budgeting? Well, you don't know what you don't know. For me, it was the "cell phone progression." I bought the Motorola brick when they were first released because I was in my car all the time, and it was immensely valuable to be able to handle 6–8 meetings a day on the road. Fast forward to the age of smart phones, and I had to be convinced to make the switch. I couldn't fathom what "better" could possibly be.

I say this because I want to reiterate that if you're in a place of frustration with budgets and why they're not working for you, it's okay. You're operating around your current level of knowledge on money, personal finance, and cash flow control. You can't yet see what the future holds, just like I couldn't conceive of how much I'd love having GPS at my fingertips, a flashlight in my pocket, songs in my ear, podcasts in my playlist, and a whole library of books in the palm of my hand. (That's right, I read all of my books right from my phone's Kindle app.)

Moving forward takes guts, and it takes learning—you can't

just snap your fingers and arrive at the perfect solution. I'll say it again: you don't know what you don't know. You're on the right track just by picking up this paper and being curious about what's out there besides budgeting.

So what can you do, if budgets don't work?

One of the first steps should be flipping that mindset. As I said, people generally turn to budgets out of fear, or a sense of lack. That's Scarcity Thinking, and it's pretty difficult to rewrite your financial circumstances when you're operating from a place of scarcity. Instead, you've got to flip the switch to abundance, or a Prosperity Mindset.

The basis of a Prosperity Mindset is that opportunities are infinite. Life is not a pie to be divided into a finite number of slices. If you can dream it, you can do it. And before you go thinking that this is just "rose colored glasses," think about how you make decisions when life feels good. You see possibilities and opportunities in everything, and you don't act because you're backed into a corner by fear.

You're also less likely to feel like there are things missing from your life, so you don't always have to spend to keep up or try to fill a void of some kind. A Prosperity Mindset is all about being content in the present and making decisions for your long-term good rather than your short-term survival.

Once you've established a positive mindset—what you can do instead of what you can't—let technology be a change agent for you. Allow yourself to be surprised by what's possible when you utilize technology that makes saving money a priority without you feeling like you're sacrificing anything in your life.

If cash flow control is a "problem area" for you, rather than restricting the flow of cash (Scarcity), instead try changing the order of operations in your personal cash flow (Prosperity). The typical order of operations is usually bills, groceries, subscriptions, and all the way at the end, there are savings… if there's anything left. The issue is that people spend way more than they think they do, and by putting savings at the end, it's not a priority.

Changing the order of operations looks like saving money FIRST, and spending the surplus. You don't have to fit all your expenses into little categories or justify what you spend. You simply decide how much of your income you want to spend each month, filter it through a Reservoir account, and put it in your checking like normal. Then, watch as your Reservoir fills up. This gives you the same dopamine hit as making a purchase, except now you're saving money to get that rush.

This is possible with one app, right on your smartphone: Currence. Currence is by invitation only and with thanks to David Mozeika. With it, you get to flip the script so that you gain the psychological benefits of seeing your Reservoir grow, rather than your garage full of goodies. We call this Income Under Management. Ditch the restrictive life of budgeting and instead choose the value of saving first.

Myth #2: I Don't Need Cash Flow Control

"Money has never made man happy, nor will it,
there is nothing in its nature to produce happiness.
The more of it one has, the more one wants"
—*Benjamin Franklin*

Remember Scrooge from *A Christmas Carol*? He's got plenty of money, yet no friends. He's so obsessed with more, more, more that he doesn't make the time to check in with the people he cares for until he loses them.

Maybe you know someone who keeps acquiring asset after asset, yet really has no cash flow because they're always seeking the next thing. Their money is all tied up.

You might be very fortunate (and hard-working) to have lots of money, so much so that you could earn and earn, spend and spend, and not really feel a thing. Saving money, budgeting, and cash flow control may not be all that important to you in this stage of life. Turning "unconscious spending into unconscious saving" might not seem like a thing you "need" to do.

The thing is, regardless of how much you have coming in, you are not on an island. (And if you act that way, you might just turn out like Scrooge before he has his change of heart.) There are people in your life who can benefit from the confidence that comes with cash flow, and thinking of them in your actions can have a positive impact on your relationships and your habits. This effect is multi-plied for them.

If, for example, you're married, your spouse could benefit from the excitement around cash flow control. This is especially true if one or both of you have some new habits you'd like to install. Plug-ging those financial leaks and replacing them with a habit of sav-ings can help you be more prepared for the future, even if you don't think it's necessary at this exact point in time. The reality is that any-thing can happen, and having an emergency/opportunity fund can prepare you for the worst-case scenario AND the best-case scenario.

If you have adult children, they might not have the same asset base as you do, and could also benefit from the confidence that cash flow control brings. That doesn't mean you have to give them assets, either. Yet modeling certain behaviors can help them adopt those behaviors to create better systems for their own cash flow.

You may have read my earlier book, *Perpetual Wealth*, and read of the benefits of having your family all on the same page about wealth building. This can be difficult when your family is all over the map, and some have overflowing wealth while others are living paycheck to paycheck. Suggesting meetings about money can lead to groans and eye rolls and maybe even arguments.

What if you could gamify the conversation around cash flow control?

When we gamify processes that aren't normally "fun," we turn them into an event that can bring more satisfaction. And since many games aren't played alone, gamifying systems can draw in new participants and family members who wouldn't otherwise join the conversation.

I recall times in my family when we all went outside and worked on a farm project. Sometimes it was overhauling the garden, sometimes picking up tree limbs after a particularly rough storm. It was hard work, but we also strove to make it fun for all involved. Tree limb collections turned into big bonfires to gather around and spend quality time together. The fire was certainly warm, and so was the feeling of accomplishment because we could all see the physical results of our labor. And because it was a family event, we could all play to our own strengths in the family clean up— big, strong family members were on giant tree limb duty while the speedy ones would race to pick up small sticks.

We all had something to contribute, and we all benefited from each other's unique skills. So many things in life seem that much sweeter when we experience them together.

So while you might not feel like you're in need of cash flow control right now, someone you love might benefit. And joining them in the process can help you, too. A rising tide lifts all boats, and you can be that catalyst.

Currence is a platform with an app and a Reservoir account that brings gamification to your table. It enables families (and friends) of all varying financial situations to compare scores without revealing personal information or exact numbers. It's not like a credit score, which really just calculates your ability to manage debt. Instead, you get to see how well your friends and family save and make progress toward their Target (minus the specific data). This keeps things fun, lightly competitive, and allows everyone in your family to support each other when appropriate.

You may be aware of Mike Michalowicz's "Profit First" concept—he teaches business owners and entrepreneurs to pull out profits before expenses because too many business owners are paying themselves what's left over, which is totally backward. Currence helps you apply this profit-first mentality to your finances, by taking your profits and putting them into your Reservoir, and then choosing how much to spend and putting that your checking account to cover expenses.

With Currence, you don't have to spend more than a few minutes getting your cash flow structure set up so that you can profit first without even thinking about it. And whether you think you need this now, being involved and bringing it to the table for your family can make a huge difference for all.

Myth #3: There's No Time

"'I don't have time' is the single most frequently given reason for living fractional, perpetually indentured lives, or not living fully or freely. Because time is life, when we say we don't have enough time, we are admitting that we don't have enough life."

— Sonia Johnson, Author

When you say that you don't have time for something, what you're really saying is that it isn't a priority, whatever "it" happens to be in a given scenario. This isn't inherently a bad thing. After all, you can't prioritize everything. That goes against the essence of the word itself. And yet, also by virtue of the word, there are some things you DO prioritize, whether you claim them or not.

Where are you putting your time? Is it where you want to put your time, or are you taking a more passive role?

If you said the latter, it might be prudent to prioritize figuring out your priorities, so you can make them a habit.

Many people say that they're motivated to "get control of money," and yet they don't take the time to do just that. Or if they do, it eludes them. This isn't for lack of time; it has more to do with it being a low priority on the totem pole. And the thing about cash flow issues is that they don't disappear, they just get more zeroes. The more you ignore them, the harder they become to ignore.

Most people put it off, though, because it's difficult to get motivated. When money is a sense of stress, fear, or anxiety, our brains just want to protect us from those feelings. And of course, it's stressful if you have to go through all your purchases and bills and other expenses. It may even make you feel shame about your money, and that's not the goal of cash flow control.

It only gets worse if you have to do it every month and spend time combing through your financial minutia in order to make sense of it. It's enough to frustrate anyone, over time.

I want you to feel PEACE when you think about your finances.

What if I told you that it didn't have to take much time at all to get some control over your cash flow? All it takes is a genuine commitment from you, and maybe 15 minutes. Not 15 minutes a day, not 15 minutes a month. Just 15 minutes, period. It's really as simple as that.

Rather than looking at all your expenses and trying to decide what you can and cannot live with, think about the big picture. What are your monthly totals? You can even use two-week totals if that's easier for you. There's no value judgment here, no micro-management of your individual transactions. Simply add up everything you pay for.

Then, using Currence, you create a Reservoir account. You redirect all your income to the Reservoir, then tell it how much to pay you. That money will hit your checking account, and you can pay all your expenses as you normally do. You don't have to change anything, and it's quick to set up.

If you earn W-2 income, think of it conceptually like when your employer holds back your taxes for you. Only in this case, what you're withholding is actually your savings or your profits. By filtering them out first, you ensure that they actually go into your savings rather than being spent unconsciously. Meanwhile, the rest goes towards your monthly spending. And you can feel free to use all of it because your savings will be covered! How's that for stress-free?

Even better, once you have it set up, you don't have to think about it. You can automate every single piece of it so that you get your expense money when you want it. And you're in control, so you can always adjust your numbers if you want to.

This idea of paying yourself first was originally coined in the 1920s by George Samuel Clason, an American entrepreneur who founded the Clason Map Company. His business was the first to produce a road atlas of the United States and Canada that was so successful, his company produced pamphlets on financial success that they distributed to major financial institutions. The pamphlets explored wisdom from ancient Babylon, what had formerly been the richest city in the world. Pay yourself first was an important principle of those pamphlets.

Even so, many people struggle to pay themselves first. And even more people feel that there's no time to do anything different or make significant changes—whether these be short-term choices or long-term time frames.

Currence isn't just wishful thinking, either. It's a proven structural solution that helps people to create massive habit changes with minimal effort and time. My friend Vince D'Addona helped a young family find time and money through the Currence app and its pay-yourself-first strategy. Just a few months after they implemented this system, they found that their reservoir already had $5,000 in it. When they saw it, they called him to ask, "Did you put that money in there?"

Vince reminded them that only they have control over their app and their account. All the good that they experienced was simply from making a shift in their order of operations and filtering their income through the Currence Reservoir.

Are you ready to pay yourself first? Consider taking the Win x3 approach. Most people are only looking for a win-win. I encourage you to look for the third win in your financial decisions. For example, can you create a win right now, a win a few months or years from now, AND a win many years from now? That's a real Win x3, and yet it might seem impossible to achieve in one fell swoop.

Another way to look at a Win x3 is the people who benefit. What if you could win, the bank where you store your money could win, and the person who helped you create the system could win? That would also be a Win x3!

Looking for ways to multiply success and benefit more people can create incredible outcomes. Currence is one of those systems that provides a win to all, and creates more conditions for success.

All it takes to have a healthier financial environment is three simple steps that take no time at all: install the app, fund the Reservoir, and link your Reservoir to your bank account. Nothing else has to change. Do you have time for that?

Myth #4: I'll Get Ahead Next Month

"If we command our wealth, we shall be rich and free. If our wealth commands us, we are poor indeed."
—Edmund Burke

This is the lie we've all told ourselves at one point or another: "I'll get ahead next month."

Usually, people say this when they've been working on their budget and things haven't been going as well in real life as they have on paper. Next month is always looking better. If you say this to yourself every month, it's time to reconsider who's in control here: you, or your money?

The thing about "next month" is that people tend to say it month after month. At what point do you say enough is enough? Why would you continue to have faith in the statement if you've said you'll get ahead month after month?

It's time to make some changes so that you're in control of your cash flow, and vice versa.

Often, people try to remedy this with a budget. The thing is, budgets don't really stop you from making this declaration, because you can always come up with ways to justify your spending. Especially if you have the funds to spend. Currence eliminates your ability to spend mindlessly by helping you put away any excess you have first.

Furthermore, I'm often surprised at how many people don't know how much money it takes to get through the month. I don't want you to analyze every single penny you spend, yet it's usually a good idea to know what your financial obligations are, and any additional expenses you may have. Thinking in terms of one large sum will help you as you navigate Currence, and prevent you from staying stuck in a state of <u>unconscious consumption</u>.

The truth is, if you want to make a habit stick, you've got to add it in now. If you think you'll wait until the perfect moment, you're going to be waiting a long time! It's okay to take small steps toward what you want to achieve. In fact, many small steps are often better than one large step and stopping.

If you've been looking for permission to stop restricting, consider this "it"! Instead, think of what you can add to your life. Can you add automation that makes it easier to save, like Currence? Can you add in additional income streams that contribute to your Reservoir? Can you add in a system that helps you save first and gain some much-desired control now, rather than later?

What would it feel like if you knew exactly what it took to get you through a month, and it didn't cause you any stress or "pain"? All you would have to do is set up simple automation. Then, whatever appears in your checking account is yours to spend. That sounds pretty painless, right? I have a feeling that if you could simplify the process, you would do it right now instead of pushing it off onto your future self. And just think of the future that would bring—one in which you have faith in your finances born of actual accomplishments. You won't have to outrun the lie that you'll get ahead next month, anymore.

My coach, Dan Sullivan, co-founder of the Strategic Coach® Program, introduced me to The Gap & The Gain®, which taught me to look forward, yet measure backwards. You can find his book at StrategicCoach.com. Measuring backwards is all about measuring your progress based on where you've come from, NOT where you're going. The latter can be paralyzing because you might not be as far as you want to be. However, when you measure backwards from where you started, you see how much incredible progress you've made! And that's encouraging.

Measuring backwards is the opposite of budgeting because you're celebrating all of the milestones you've already achieved as opposed to how many you've yet to accomplish. Budgeting forces you to look ahead in a race while you're "behind," with little hope of catching up. It's no wonder people struggle with budgeting. Yet with Currence, you get to see this incredible Reservoir you're building from the ground up, which builds faith into your finances. This enables you to get ahead not just next month but for your entire life.

Myth #5: Savers Are Losers

"It is not necessary to do extraordinary things to get extraordinary results."

—*Warren Buffett*

Robert Kiyosaki of *Rich Dad, Poor Dad* fame says savers are losers. I say that saving saves families. So which is it?

Well, I'll admit that Robert is right if you see "savings" as a noun or an account. It's true that if all you do is store money in a bank that earns less than inflation, you are technically losing money.

Yet if you see "savings" as a verb, you'll realize that the act of putting money away can actually save you and your family from heartache AND take advantage of opportunities.

Cash is what makes the world go around, even for Robert Kiyosaki. The best investments require lump sums of capital. And in many cases, emergencies can require lump sums, too. Your life, however, operates monthly. You don't earn income as fast as you can employ it, which suggests that somewhere, somehow you have to store money away until you hit a target of some sort.

Converting these monthly savings into a lump sum that you can use to pursue good investments requires discipline. Yuck! And to try and do this alone, with no help? Depressing!

Like in Myth #2, having people walk alongside you on the journey can make everything more fun. In fact, a community can bring you a sense of peace and confidence to know that you're not in uncharted terrain—you're on a pilgrimage. What if you could be in a community of Simplified Savers who were Automating Assets so they could install Faith in their Finances?

This community exists, and it's made up of financial advisors and their clients who are walking this journey together. And they can help you, too. It's called the Prosperity Economics Movement.

If you're ready to embark on the journey, it all begins with you. This is the same thing I said to myself when my husband, Todd Langford, and I co-founded the non-profit. Everything I do for myself, I do for my clients, and I hope they do it for their families and team members. I live the advice that I give every single day because I believe in it's power. It has helped me, my family, and the countless families I serve time and time again.

I also keep in mind every other advisor out there in this space and their clientele in the hopes that the ever-widening ripple effect goes on in perpetuity. This is my passion and my mission: to prevent millions of wasted lives, and dollars, by sharing this message.

I want to give as abundantly as I can so that everyone can have this knowledge and these resources if they so choose.

It's so easy to waste money on all sorts of things. It's not my place to judge, as one man's trash is another's treasure. Yet I can't help but think that we humans spend a little too much time regretting the purchases we've made. While some of this is inevitable, I feel like the deeper lesson is that stuff and things only bring temporary reprieve. In the grand scheme of things, it is experiences and memories that have value to us. While some experiences do have price tags, that's not always the case.

In order to prevent millions of wasted dollars (and lives), it's important to define what's truly important to you. Don't spend your dollars based on what others deem valuable. Determine what's important to you and your family and stick to that. The money that you save in the short term becomes valuable in the long term, which can then be used toward things that really matter to you.

If you're ready to make this change, you can ask to be invited to Currence, fund your Reservoir, and link your accounts. That's all it takes to create <u>unconscious savings</u>. Then, if you like what you experience, invite others into the community right from the app. You, your family, and your friends can all work toward building a savings habit first so that you then have the capital to invest. And one at a time, we can change the world.

PART 2: SAVE OR PAY OFF DEBT?

NOT ALL FINANCIAL QUESTIONS are mathematical or numerical questions, even if they involve numbers. Financial progress isn't just a "science," it's also an art, and it takes nuance to find the right solution. After all, there's more to our financial lives than just the numbers. There are psychological factors at play that have to do with how, when, and where we were raised, and by whom, as well as all of the life events we've experienced between now and then. Humans carry baggage (good or not) that impacts the financial, sometimes to interesting results. And so, on occasion, our questions–and the resulting strategies–-must be as unique as our circumstances. If you want to Google the answers, your mileage may vary.

For many adults, one of the primary questions financial advisors hear is, "Should I save first, or pay off the debt first?" This question isn't a numbers question, it's a psychological one. So while you can approach it as a science and seek the answer based on pure financial efficiency, it's worth noting that sometimes the even better solution is the one that provides peace of mind. For others, there may even be a middle ground.

Yet, the reality stands—no calculator system in the world can measure peace of mind or psychological motivation. So although the Truth Concepts calculator suite can tell you the whole truth about all things financial, there's no way to measure the immeasurable. Instead, it's up to you to be honest with yourself—and an advisor, if you're working with one—to uncover your personal desires and motivations. That way, the right solution can surface, not just any solution.

So what makes mathematical sense, and what makes emotional sense? Well, if you break down the pure economics, then paying off credit card debt certainly makes sense. However, from an emotional standpoint, it can be difficult to funnel so much energy into debt repayment and have nothing "in the bank."

That being said, we'd like to suggest that a good "middle ground" is typically to do BOTH. You can make an effort to save AND pay off debt at the same time, in order to avoid going into further debt if an emergency should arise. This is an option that makes both financial and emotional sense for many people.

Additionally, you get what you focus on. So if all your focus is on "paying off debt," there is a chance you'll go down a path that leads to more debt. By instead focusing on saving money first, with an added goal of debt reduction, your main focus is on building. By keeping your attention aimed at a target of growth, that's the path you can expect to stay on. Furthermore, the earlier you start saving, even in small amounts, the sooner you benefit from the compound interest curve. After all, the more money you have, the more money you earn through interest and dividends. The sooner you start, the more time you get to compound.

The cost of delaying your savings is "opportunity cost." This is represented by the compounding interest you would lose out on for every month you delay saving money. You could start saving today, and you'll certainly get to benefit from compounding every day after, yet you'll never recoup the interest you could have earned. While there's no use dwelling on what that could be, it serves as a good reminder to get started.

All of this is to say that there are many paths that you can take when you face the question of debt vs. savings. And ultimately, you should do what feels good to you. What gives one person peace of mind might not give you peace of mind, and peace should be one of your primary objectives.

With this in mind, let's look at various ways to pay down debt. Some are more mathematically favorable, while others are more psychologically favorable. Hopefully, within these methods, you'll find something that inspires and empowers you to tackle your debt. And in the meantime, we hope you can save, too.

How Do You Pay Off Debt?

While we certainly have our opinions, there are many strategies for debt repayment. We've compiled what we believe, in our opinion, are the best strategies for debt repayment, both numerical/mathematical and psychological/behavioral. Within those two categories are a variety of methods:

1. Effective Mathematical Solutions: Debt Avalanche, Intra-Family Loans
2. Effective Psychological Solutions: Debt Snowball, Cash Flow Index

Before you can start with one of those strategies, however, you've got to get a good snapshot of what you're working with. This means gathering all the data on your current financial picture, then it's time to get organized.

You can start by making a list of all the debt that you owe—consumer debt, loans, medical bills, and any other balance you're trying to pay down. Make note of the total debt amount, the current interest rate, and the minimum payment. This will help you if you want to try doing your own math on any of these strategies to find your favorite.

Some would suggest creating a budget, though we disagree with this common advice. The reason budgeting doesn't work is because it's too restrictive. While you'll find some people who can be successful budgeters, you'll find even more who feel a deep sense of shame around budgeting. Instead, we encourage people to save first, and then spend the rest.

You don't have to save much to do this, either. This is just as effective in moving the needle if you can only save $20 as it is if you can save $2,000 a month. You're making forward progress, and that counts when you've previously been saving $0. You'll have to have some knowledge about your obligatory spending, yet that still doesn't mean you have to "budget" in the typical sense. Instead, you can monitor where and what you're spending money on, and then make changes according to your values and objectives.

Effectively, in the order of operations, you'll save what you want to save first, pay your bills and debts second, and then if there's anything remaining, you're free to spend it. This is far less restrictive than a typical budget and allows you to align your habits to your values.

If you're deliberating how to allocate your dollars to saving or spending, here are some other things to consider:

- Do you have high-interest consumer debt? Mathematically speaking (which we'll discuss in more depth shortly) these are often the debts you want to tackle first. After all, they're pure interest cost.

- What does your current emergency/opportunity fund look like? Do you have a few months worth of expenses saved? If not, you may want to pause additional debt payments until you've created more of a cushion for yourself. That way you don't go into further debt in an emergency.

- Ultimately, what's going to make you feel most accomplished?

Paying down your debt is a personal decision, and there's no right or wrong answer. The right choice is the one that helps you make progress. If you're not making progress, try reevaluating and tackling a different strategy.

Here are some additional tips for saving money AND paying down debt:

- Create financial objectives for yourself. Don't be afraid to look at the bigger picture and dream big. The more you focus on the positive aspects of your journey, the more apparent the positive aspects of your journey will be.

- Automate your systems. You can make your savings AND your spending automatic so that you don't have to think about it. It will just happen! This is especially helpful if you have trouble remembering to make payments.

- Align your spending with your values. By knowing where your money goes, you can make choices to cut out expenses that no longer have a role in your greater vision.

- Find ways to increase your income. Get a side hustle, raise your prices—by creating extra income, you can either increase your savings capability, your debt repayment ability, or both!

- Work with a professional. Not every financial advisor offers debt services, though some do. Just be sure you have a good understanding of how they get paid for those services. Even non-profit debt or credit consultants typically have a fee. That fee can be worth it, just be sure you know what it is.

- Work with a credit counseling agency. Credit counselors can help you identify a good strategy, negotiate your debts with creditors, and even help you reduce interest costs.

Once you have a good idea of where you're at now, and where you want to go, it's time to determine which strategy is going to work best for you.

1. Debt Avalanche (Mathematically Effective)

The debt avalanche is a very common debt repayment strategy, and financially speaking, one of the most effective methods. That's because it's all about tackling the highest interest-rate debt first.

Here is an example of how the debt avalanche method works:

Say you have three debts:

- A credit card with a balance of $5,000 and an interest rate of 20%
- Student loans with a balance of $10,000 and an interest rate of 6%
- A car loan with a balance of $15,000 and an interest rate of 4%

Once you know what you're working with, it's time to determine what order to pay them in. With a debt avalanche strategy, your objective is to eliminate the most interest cost. Therefore, you want to tackle the highest interest rate first. For your other debt, you need only make minimum payments in the meantime.

In this case, you'll want to pay the credit card debt first. Even though it has the lowest balance, the interest rate is going to pose the biggest problem. It's also worth noting that your student loans and car loans are designed to be paid off over a certain period of time, while your credit card is not. So a minimum payment on those loans will make a lot more traction than a minimum credit card payment.

Now it's time to determine how much money you have to put toward your debt. Subtract the minimum payments you'll be making from that total, and what's leftover is going to go to the credit card. You want to pay as much as possible on the credit card, until it's completely paid off. Then, just move to the next highest interest rate–in this case, the student loan–until it's also paid off. Continue until you're debt-free.

Most people consider this to be one of the most effective methods, because you're reducing the greatest interest cost first. However, because this doesn't account for the actual volume of debt, it can sometimes be difficult to gauge progress. For example, if you have $1,000 of debt with a 20% interest rate and $10,000 at 10%, you're racking up a much higher volume of interest on the $10,000, even at a lower rate. This can make progress seem slow, or even "backward," and therefore discouraging.

So remember to take into account the volume of interest in addition to the interest rate. That may change how you decide to approach the debt.

2. Intra-Family Loan

You might also consider an intra-family loan. In other words, asking a parent, grandparent, sibling, or other family member to help you consolidate your debt into one single loan. If you have many debts with high-interest rates, consolidating can provide you with significant savings. Additionally, getting this financed through a family banking system can provide additional flexibility.

However, intra-family loans can also come with complicated emotional challenges, and should not be entered into without proper documentation. Making things official and doing it by the book can keep emotions to a minimum. At the very least, it sets a legal precedent by having paperwork documenting the loan terms. (And yes, there should be a strategy in place for what happens if you default on the loan. This makes it fair and safe for the family member providing the financing.)

Here is an example: Your grandparents have money sitting in savings at 2%. You have credit card debt at 24%. Your grandparents could lend you the money at 12%, reducing your interest cost by 50% and increasing your grandparent's results by 500% as you can see in the figure below.

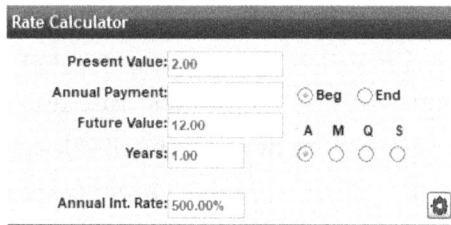

Don't just take our word for it though, let's examine it with real numbers. Say your grandparents have $100,000 in that savings account. If the account is earning 2% interest, that's an annual increase of $2,000.

If you wanted to make interest only payments on the loan for the first year, that would mean a $12,000 annual payment. If you subtract the $2,000 interest from this, you get $10,000, which is how much additional interest your grandparents earn from the loan. This is quite literally 5 times what they would earn without the loan, or 500%.

It is important to note, in this case, that the interest on the loan would be considered income, and therefore would be taxable. However, even with taxes, the grandparents in this case will still have a greater end result.

For the "you" in this scenario, it's important to actually make more than interest-only payments if you're serious about getting out of debt. Reducing the interest rate so significantly should help. The ideal way to make progress in this case is to at least pay what you were already paying on the credit cards you've consolidated, if not more. That way you can get the debt taken care of as fast as possible.

The reason intra-family loans tend to be better than a debt consolidation company is three-fold. First, you get to benefit someone you know personally by boosting their earned interest. And second, you're much more likely to get a reasonable interest rate with a family member who knows you than you are with a major loan servicer. And three, keeping a loan in the family, even with the appropriate paperwork, avoids impacting your credit score through credit checks, let alone a large loan appearing on your report.

3. Debt Snowball (Psychologically Effective)

The debt snowball is, in a way, the inverse of the debt avalanche. While the debt avalanche focuses on interest rates, the debt snowball focuses on your debt balances. The idea is to pay off the SMALLEST debt first, so that you can feel a sense of accomplishment and victory early in the process.

As you pay off the smallest debt, you take the payment and add it to the next largest. This way, you're paying off specific balances quickly, leaving the toughest for last. This is so psychologically effective because it provides gratification as fast as possible.

And typically, when people have early success, they're motivated to keep the momentum of that success.

So let's look at some numbers to show how the debt snowball works in practice.

Say you have three debts:

- Credit card debt with a balance of $5,000 and an interest rate of 20%
- Student loan debt with a balance of $10,000 and an interest rate of 6%
- Car loan debt with a balance of $15,000 and an interest rate of 4%

Once you've created a list of your debts, identify the smallest balance. In this case, it's the $5,000 with an interest rate of 20%. Then, you'll identify the minimum payments of each credit card or loan, and add them up. From that sum, identify how much more money you can contribute to your debt each month. Once you do that, you're going to pay the minimum payment on everything except for the smallest balance. On the smallest balance, you'll pay as much as you possibly can each month until it's paid off.

Some people criticize this method because it doesn't necessarily reduce your interest costs. That being said, you won't reduce your interest costs with inaction, either. So if the debt avalanche feels demotivating for you, don't sweat it. The best solution is going to be the one that you can stick to. If you're motivated by seeing your balances paid down, ignore the interest cost debate. By making consistent payments, the snowball method WILL work if you keep at it. And paying down your debt is better than not.

4. Cash Flow Index (Psychologically Effective)

The Cash Flow Index (CFI) method is a debt repayment strategy that prioritizes your debts based on their impact on your cash flow. This means that you will pay off the debts that are costing you the most money each month first. In other words, rather than looking at your interest RATE or your balances, you're looking at the efficiency of the loans, based on the minimum payment and the volume of the loan.

The CFI measures the efficiency of your debt—the higher the number, the more efficient that debt is, and the less you have to worry about it. For example, if you have a high minimum payment with a low debt balance, this is actually an inefficient loan because you're probably paying more interest. Credit cards are usually inefficient because the minimum payment is designed to barely outpace the accumulated interest. You certainly CAN pay off a credit card with the minimum payment, but it might take you 10 years if you put nothing else on the card.

So for the CFI method, you're tackling your low-efficiency debt first. That way you can save some interest cost, reduce your total minimum payments, and make traction on your repayment with relative ease.

To calculate the CFI for each debt, you will need to divide the balance of the debt by the minimum monthly payment.

For example, let's say you have three debts:

- Credit card debt with a balance of $5,000 and a minimum monthly payment of $200.
- Student loan debt with a balance of $10,000 and a minimum monthly payment of $100.
- Car loan debt with a balance of $15,000 and a minimum monthly payment of $300.

To calculate the CFI for each debt, we would divide the balance by the minimum monthly payment.

- Credit card debt: $5,000 / $200 = 25
- Student loan debt: $10,000 / $100 = 100
- Car loan debt: $15,000 / $300 = 50

Just like with all other repayment strategies, you'll continue making minimum payments on your low priority debts, while paying as much as possible to the priority debt. In this case, the priority is the credit card, which is the least efficient. Although it doesn't have the highest minimum payment, its payment relative to the balance is high, which signals high-interest costs.

Based on this method, after you pay the credit card off, you would tackle the car loan next, then the student loans.

This is psychologically effective, because as with the debt snowball method, you're tackling debts in a manner that allows for "quick" victories. If you're motivated by success, this can be a good method to adopt.

Other Ideas for Debt Reduction

The above strategies are useful for approaching the repayment of your debt, yet that's not necessarily all there is to debt reduction and saving money. In addition to HOW to pay your debt, there are also things you can do to reduce your debt costs.

These methods can take a bit of work and determination (like calling your credit card companies), though the end result can make a big difference in your overall results. Here are some options to consider, and HOW they can move the needle in your favor.

Reduce your Interest Rate

In addition to a solid repayment strategy, reducing your interest rates whenever possible can help you get debt paid off faster. And, of course, with less interest cost. So how do you go about reducing your interest rates? You've got to call your credit card companies. And sometimes you have to be persistent and call until you get an answer you like.

While this may not sound like an appealing strategy, you may change your mind when you see just how big the impact can be. In the Figure below, we've illustrated a $10,000 credit card balance at an interest rate of 24% inside of the Loan Analysis calculator from Truth Concepts. Say you were committed to paying it off in 24 months, the below amortization schedule is what you can expect.

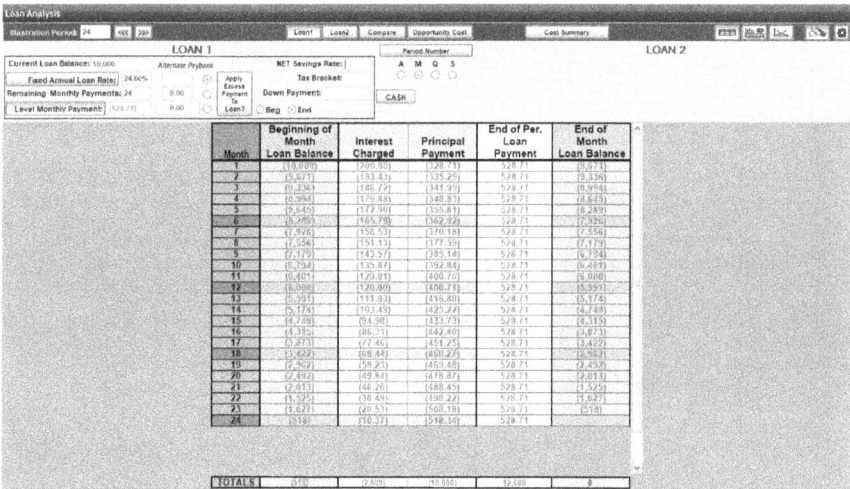

If, by calling your credit card company diligently, you were able to have them reduce the interest rate to 12%, then you could reduce your payment from $528.71 to $470.73 and still pay off your debt on the exact same schedule. (See the chart at the top of the next page.)

You may be thinking: "Yeah, but shouldn't I keep paying the $528 to reduce the debt faster?" The answer to that is that absolutely you CAN. In fact, if you look at the figure below, you'll be able to pay the debt off in 22 months instead of 24. (See the second chart on the next page.)

Yet whether or not you "should" do is another thing altogether. We're not going to presume, yet think of it this way. You've already committed to paying off the card in two years with a higher interest rate. The difference is just about $60 ($57.98 to be exact), so what would happen if you saved that?

If you saved that under your mattress (not earning interest), you'd have $1,392 in savings AND a paid off credit card in just

24 months. Otherwise, you could have a paid off credit card in 22 months and NO savings.

Future Value Calculator

Present Value: 0.00
Monthly Payment: 57.98   ⊙ Beg   ○ End
Annual Int. Rate: 0.00%   A   M   Q   S
Months: 24.00   ○   ⊙   ○   ○

Future Value: 1,392

And if you were able to save that $57.98 into an interest earning account, you'd have even more. A mere 2% account would inch your savings up by about $30.

Future Value Calculator

Present Value: 0.00
Monthly Payment: 57.98   ⊙ Beg   ○ End
Annual Int. Rate: 2.00%   A   M   Q   S
Months: 24.00   ○   ⊙   ○   ○

Future Value: 1,421

This is the power of saving AND paying debt, as opposed to just paying down your debt and saving later. You can accomplish two objectives and end up all the better for it by the end of the journey. And if you can reduce your interest rate, you can increase your savings capability even more without interrupting your repayment schedule at all. Or, if you're really craving that peace of mind that comes with a paid-off card, you can knock a few months off of the repayment schedule.

Using Life Insurance Cash Value Loans

In addition to intra-family loans, you can also use cash value loans against a whole life insurance policy to help pay down your debt. This can either be from a family member OR if you have your own life insurance policy, you can actually take your own loan to pay down your debt.

It's important to note that when you're borrowing money FROM the life insurance company, AGAINST your cash value, you're not "getting out of debt." You may be transferring your debt, however, the debt is still very much there. The benefit of doing this, however, is that you can generally get a much more favorable interest rate from your insurance company than your credit card company, AND you have the added flexibility of life insurance loans in general.

For example, if you wanted some time to establish additional cash flow, you could make interest only payments on your cash value loan for a few months or years. You'd still have the debt, of course, yet some added flexibility to get your cash flow in order. This would also improve your credit, since the loan wouldn't be reported to credit agencies—to them, it would appear as if you've paid your debts.

Another note of importance: you're not paying yourself interest when you take a life insurance loan. You are paying the assigned interest rate to the life insurance company, whose money you're borrowing. The reason there's confusion is because you can pay the loan back at a higher interest rate annually, and if you haven't paid your maximum allotted PUAs, the difference can be assigned to your policy as if it were a PUA contribution. So if you paid a 6% loan at 8%, that 2% could be contributed to your cash value as a PUA.

We'll come back to this idea of debt repayment with whole life insurance, yet first, let's talk about how to get started with a whole life insurance policy for savings, too.

Buying Whole Life Insurance

As stated at the beginning of this section, building savings is an important step to do alongside paying off debt. After your Emergency fund is "complete," starting a Whole Life Insurance policy to store your Opportunity Fund is the most efficient way to continue building and storing your cash over the course of your whole life, hence the name of the product. This is a necessary step to participating in the policy loan provision of life insurance.

If you do not yet have a whole life insurance policy, we recommend that you only use dividend-paying whole life insurance from a mutual company, rather than a public-stock life insurance company. This is the key to receiving interest and dividends, which you do as a partial owner of the mutual company you sign a contract with. Once you have as much whole life insurance as you can get with your cash flow, we recommend buying additional term insurance to fulfill your Human Life Value (HLV). We like to approach it from a top-down, bottom-up standpoint, as we'll explain below.

Top-Down:

The "top" of this equation starts with identifying your HLV (Human Life Value) which is mathematically determined as a factor of your income. In general, 15 to 30 times your income (or 1 times your gross worth) is the maximum amount of death benefit you can qualify for with the whole life insurance company.

If you don't have your own income—stay-at-home spouses, for example—you can usually qualify for about half of what your spouse can. And if you're a child, you generally qualify for about a quarter of what the higher-earning parent can qualify for.

Identifying the top empowers you to understand just how much life insurance you can get. That doesn't necessarily mean you have to buy that much whole life insurance. In fact, many people can't start out funding their HLV with whole life insurance alone. This is where the "bottom" of the equation comes into play. Then you fund the difference between the smaller Whole life policy and your Human Life Value with convertible term life insurance.

Bottom-Up:
Once you've identified how much you CAN get, it's time to figure out what you're actually capable of putting away each month or year. You want this to be a consistent number that you can reliably pay, like from the primary breadwinner's income. And if that's the case, then that's the person you'll insure.

The number you determine you can save, based on your cash flow, will be the primary breadwinner's whole life insurance premium. If you have bonus money that's less consistently reliable, you can use that to boost your PUAs (paid-up additions). PUAs allow you to build even more cash for opportunities.

Whole Life Insurance Loans for Debt Repayment

Once you have cash value built up, which does take time, you can use the policy loan provision to finance anything you want, including to consolidate your debt under a more favorable interest rate. This is a legitimate strategy, so long as you continue to pay your cash value loan. It doesn't help if you merely transfer one debt for another and then default on it.

So let's look at the 24% credit card from earlier. Say you called your credit card company, and the best that they can do is the 12% from our earlier example. You decide to check out other options, and see that your life insurance company has a current loan rate of 8%. You decide to pay down your credit card with a life insurance loan, and choose to keep your loan payments the same. By doing this, you're able to pay the balance in 21 months instead of 24, or even 22 if you had taken the credit card company's offer of 12%.

In fact, the 21st month would only require a payment of about $150, making the final month particularly easy on the wallet.

Alternately, if you wanted to, you could continue to pay the loan over the same 24 month period you planned initially, and save the difference. In a simple savings account, earning 2%, you could have almost $2,000 saved. You could contribute this to your whole life insurance premium as PUAs, or you could simply keep it in an account on the side for smaller, more immediate emergencies.

Future Value Calculator

Present Value:	0.00
Monthly Payment:	76.44 ⊙ Beg ○ End
Annual Int. Rate:	2.00% A M Q S
Months:	24.00 [Adj] ○ ⊙ ○ ○
Future Value:	1,873

Does Life Insurance Keep Earning Dividends?

One of the many reasons whole life insurance is so efficient when it comes to financing is that you get to partake in the interest and dividends on the full amount of your cash value, whether or not you have a loan out. (This is true, even for direct recognition loans, which we'll cover.) If your emergency/opportunity fund is saved at the bank, you would have to withdraw those funds, losing some of the compounding effect—when your interest earns interest. Money you withdraw is also money you can never "put back" into the account, you'll always be playing catch up.

Even so, dividends and interest shouldn't be factored into the savings and debt reduction equation of whole life insurance. While they're certainly a benefit, your account is going to earn interest and dividends regardless of what you do, or don't do, in the account. This is a common misconception, and one we want to correct!

First, let's talk about compound interest, which also affects your loans.

What's the Difference Between Compounding or Simple Interest?

Investopedia explains Compound Interest as "the interest on savings calculated on both the initial principal and the accumulated interest from previous periods." Investopedia explains Simple Interest by saying, "Simple interest is based on the original principal amount of a loan or deposit."

While many people can wrap their heads around the idea of compounding interest on their savings, people also erroneously believe that loans are the opposite. After all, if you have a declining balance, how can the interest possibly compound?

The answer is that those loans compound between payments, and your payments are designed to decrease your balance based on pre-calculated compounding.

For example, if your payment frequency is less than your compounding frequency, compound interest occurs between payments. So if you pay monthly, but your financial institution (bank or insurance company) computes interest daily, as most do, then compounding occurs between your monthly payments every single day.

Most bank loans charge compound interest because the interest frequency is daily. Meanwhile, payment frequency is monthly, therefore there is interest charged on interest daily as it accrues throughout the month. Then the monthly payment wipes out the accrued interest and some principal, and the process starts again. This is by design.

Are Interest Rates on Life Insurance Loans Compound or Simple?

In the same fashion, a life insurance loan is most often compounded daily and the payments are made either monthly or annually, so it too is a "compound interest loan." However, many people erroneously consider it to be simple interest.

For example, if a company's APR is 5.5%, then the daily rate (because they compound daily, like most banks) is 0.014669% (or 0.00014669). If you multiply 0.00014669 by the days in a year (365), it equals 0.05354185 or 5.35%.

So why is the sum of the daily rates (5.35%) less than the stated annual rate of 5.5%? The answer is that 5.5% is the actual APR (just like at a bank), and takes into account the daily compounding that has occurred. So what looks and feels like simple interest is actually compound interest.

By the same token, many people discuss credit card monthly credit card charges as if the monthly charge can simply be added up to make the sum of the annual interest (like 1% a month is equal to 12% a year, or 1.5% a month is equal to 18%). Yet in reality, those monthly charges do compound, and 1.5% is actually 19.56% in practice; it's not just 18%.

To say a loan with a life insurance company is simple interest and not compound interest is entirely false. If it were true, you wouldn't get credit back (at interest) for making loan payments in advance vs. in arrears.

Direct Recognition Loans vs. Non-Direct Recognition Loans

When trying to explain policy loans, and Direct Recognition vs. Non-Direct Recognition life insurance companies, we like to begin with a discussion of ownership. In a mutual insurance company, policyholders are the owners of the company. Whole life insurance is not like car insurance, home insurance, or other types of property insurance where you funnel money in and may never see it again. Yet life insurance frequently gets lumped together with all other insurance by agents and clients alike.

Yet when you're an owner of a whole life insurance policy with a mutual company, you're a partial owner of that insurance company. When you understand this, it becomes clear that the success of the insurance company is in your best interest. The company's success is your success, and corresponds to the dividends you receive. It's a good thing when your life insurance company invests conservatively and makes decisions that are both profitable and balanced. This keeps life insurance coverage intact and keeps mutual companies mutual (which means you and your fellow policyholders continue to receive dividends).

The reason it's important to pay policy loans back is not that you get to magically funnel more money into your cash value. It's important because you're being a good steward of "your" company. It's in your best interest to replenish the company's general portfolio—which is the source of your policy loan—and contribute to the company's success. (Not to mention, the company has your cash value ear-marked if you don't pay.)

Why Do PolicyHolders Get Dividends?

Dividends, too, are frequently oversimplified as a return of premium. While this is true from an IRS perspective, there's more to dividends than that. Dividends get paid to policyholders because policyholders own the life insurance company. Therefore, they get to partake in the profits of the company. In order for a mutual company to stay mutual, it must distribute ALL of its profits.

Knowing that companies loan money from the general portfolio, this begs the question—how are dividends distributed to the many owners, even if some of them have loans and some don't? Don't the loans reduce what the company can invest and earn in the marketplace? Yes.

And is that fair? Well, only if those with loans are paying for it. If someone reduces the investment potential of the company, the most equitable solution is that the person or people who did so pay for that. Otherwise, every policyholder ends up affected by those with loans.

In order for the loan to not hurt the rest of the life insurance policies, the loan rate has to be at least what the portfolio rate is. Otherwise, everyone who has a policy with the company is paying for this person's loan. This is part of the logic behind Non-Direct Recognition companies, which have variable interest rates.

Why Take a Loan in the First Place?

The reality is, you don't have to take a policy loan against your cash value. You can liquidate your policy (withdraw) if you don't want to pay interest. And if your main objective is to eliminate debt, shouldn't you at least consider liquidating? Well... let's explore that.

If the loan rate is 5%, and the net IRR (Internal Rate of Return) on the general portfolio is 4%, from a pure economics standpoint, would it be better to borrow or liquidate? The answer would be to liquidate: because why would you borrow at 5% to earn 4% when you can liquidate and lose out on 4% on a fraction of your total cash value? From a pure economics standpoint, over the course of a year, it would be better to lose 4% instead of paying 5%.

However, there's a problem. And that is: you can't put that money that you liquidate back. So you're not losing 4% on your liquidation temporarily, you're losing 4% on that amount forever. That is going to be more impactful to your cash value over time than taking the loan and paying it back.

Say you liquidate $50,000. You're not JUST losing $2,000 (4%) over a year's time frame. You can't put that money back, so you're losing out on all the future compounding, too. After five years that $50,000 would have grown to be $60,833. Over ten years, it would have been $74,012. Borrowing against the cash value allows you to pay a percentage now to get uninterrupted compounding growth indefinitely.

The Whole Truth About Direct Recognition Companies

The next piece of this discussion is Direct Recognition companies. In conversations about life insurance and policy loans, "recognition" refers to how the insurance companies pay dividends in relation to the policy loan. Direct Recognition loans get a bad rap by people who don't understand how or why they work. They're often framed as a rip-off; the most common myth being that any money that is collateralized will not earn any dividends. However, in all honesty, Direct Recognition companies are more "fair" to policy-holders than Non-Direct Recognition.

Whenever you have a fixed loan rate with an insurance company, it will always be a Direct Recognition loan. Let's say you have a fixed loan rate of 6%. What happens, then, if the insurance company's portfolio earnings skyrocketed to 20% and they have their money loaned out at 6%? Well, with Direct Recognition, the insurance company pays dividends on any collateralized dollars relative to the loan rate.

Usually, this is only a 1% differential. So with a loan at 6%, the dividend on what you're borrowing would be capped at 5%. The rest of your cash value would earn dividends as usual. This is fair, because the money the company loans to you could have been earning 20%. If they paid you a dividend based on that 20%, regardless of your outstanding loans, that's as if other policyholders are paying out of their pockets.

What often gets ignored is the potential upside to Direct Recognition. If the declared dividend rate is well below your fixed loan rate, you actually have a chance of receiving a higher interest rate on your collateralized cash value. For example, if you're paying 8% and the portfolio is only earning 1%, the company must still be fair. After all, your loan is generating more profit for the company—they have a guaranteed 8% for their general portfolio.

So in reality, Direct Recognition is really about distributing dividends in a way that is proportionate to policyholders.

Non-Direct Recognition Companies

Variable loan rates, on the other hand, can be Direct or Non-Direct, depending on the company. Say a Non-Direct Recognition company is earning 8% on their general portfolio, while charging 6% for policy loans, and the portfolio earnings creep up to 10%. They can move the loan interest rate up to match the portfolio rate. However, most companies can only raise the rate around a quarter of a point a year. So if the portfolio earnings jump a few points, and the loan rate does not, all the policyholders are affected by that regardless of whether or not they have a loan.

So while Non-Direct Recognition may seem like a better deal because they pay the same proportion of dividend on all cash value, this also means that all policyholders are affected even if they don't have a loan.

So which is better? Well, it may surprise you to know that the long-term difference between Direct and Non-Direct Recognition companies, in reality, is not that big. Over 30 years, dividend-earning policies will have similar growth trajectories regardless of Direct or Non-Direct Recognition.

This all boils down to the simple fact that there are no deals in the life insurance industry. Everything is a trade-off between cost and risk. Both Direct and Non-Direct make trade-offs that balance out the dividend portion so that the company is sustainable.

Variable interest rates balance cost and risk by adjusting the loan rate to match what's happening in the portfolio. The fixed interest rates companies balance cost and risk by paying dividends according to policy loans. Neither is better than the other in the grand scheme of things—they're just different.

As a policyholder and part-owner of the insurance company, what should matter most to you is that the company is managed in a way that is sustainable and fair. The checks and balances are not to limit you or punish you for taking loans, they're to keep the company afloat and ensure that their track record of paying dividends can continue.

Both Direct and Non-Direct Recognition companies operate in a way that benefits the company—and therefore the YOU as the policyholder. Getting too caught up in projections and analysis paralysis will only keep your client from starting a policy. The sooner you get started, the sooner you have coverage and cash value in place.

How Will You Tackle Your Savings Versus Your Debt?

Now that you have some strategies in mind, how will you approach your debt and savings? Hopefully, you can see the benefit to saving all along the way, even as you tackle your debt. Rest assured that no matter what approach you take, you're making traction toward your objectives.

PART 3: CREDIT IMPROVEMENT

IF YOU'VE GOT SIGNIFICANT DEBT, you might not like to think too deeply about your credit score. There's a good chance you're not happy with the number. However, that one little number can significantly impact your future opportunities. The thing about debt is that as much as we don't want to have debt, some debt is necessary. It helps us get car loans, mortgages, and even business financing, which are all GOOD things.

On the flip side, a good credit score can also give us access to things that don't seem as good, like credit cards. While we're not going to suggest that credit cards are GOOD, point blank, they can be useful tools when used properly. They shouldn't be something to fear. However, because of the way society approaches credit cards, they remain a tricky space. It's tempting to use them as an emergency/opportunity fund, which is how people tend to get into debt that they struggle to get out of.

Learning how to manage your credit for a good score can help you stay out of consumer debt, AND it can give you even better financing options in the future. A good credit score unlocks good interest rate opportunities down the line, meaning significant savings on "good" debt, like a mortgage.

We know and like the work Uqual.com does. They provide credit consultations and help clean up credit reports which will help you get lower interest rates in the future.

However, if you're wanting the tools and tips to get started cleaning up your credit on your own, keep reading. We'll tell you what you want to know about keeping your credit score in good standing, so you can start boosting your credit score today.

The Components of a Credit Score

Your credit score is a reflection of your ability to use credit wisely—according to the Credit Bureaus' standards. Credit reporting bureaus use your history of using and managing debt to determine a number—your credit score—which can signal to future lenders whether you'd be able to reliably manage another debt. The higher your credit score, the more likely you are to get approved for new loans and lines of credit, and the better interest rate you're likely to get.

If you're trying to accomplish financial objectives like paying off debt or saving money, you might not think of your credit score as something important. However, a good credit score can open a lot of doors for you down the road, and it takes time to build a good score. You don't want to wait until you're ready to apply for something significant, like a home, to start thinking about your credit score.

Credit History

While technically all of your credit data is your "history," what this refers to on your credit report is how long you've been working to establish your credit score. The longer your history, the better your score. After all, the more data the credit bureaus have, the more accurately they can represent you. They're looking for patterns in your credit usage overall. If you had a blip of high credit usage in college, yet you've kept your balances low in the following years, that blip likely won't have a significant impact on your score.

This is why it's important to start establishing your credit as early as possible. You want a proven track record over many years that you're reliable. And if you're concerned that your history isn't reliable, you want plenty of time to show that you've improved!

Do note: transferring a balance from one credit card to another causes a loss of that history. Be aware of tempting offers to jump to new cards with 0% interest for a year if you are trying to establish a good payment history.

Payment History

Part of a reliable track record is showing that you can make your payments on time. Ideally, that means 100% on-time payments for all of your accounts. If you aren't there now, you want to aim for 100% from this point forward.

On-time payments have a major impact on your overall score, because ultimately that's what lenders want to see: that you can pay them by the due date. Even if you have high balances (which can reflect negatively on your score), proving that you can make the payments on time shows that you're not over-extended.

Credit Usage and Total Amount Owed

Next, credit bureaus want to know how much you owe, and how much of your credit limit you've used. This can show if you're overextended, and the total amount owed is used to calculate your debt-to-income ratio.

If you have a lot of debt comparative to your income, this can reflect negatively on your score. This is just one more reason to pay down your debt, especially your consumer debt. Likewise, if you are using over a certain percentage of your total credit limit, this can reflect negatively on your score. In general, you want to aim for using less than 50% of your total credit limit on consumer accounts. The lower you can get that percentage the better.

For example, if you have a total credit limit of $10,000, you want to carry a balance of $5,000 or less from month to month.

New Credit

Every time you open a new credit account, that impacts your score negatively. The reason this is an automatic "ding" is because the account is new, and therefore there's no data on whether or not you can manage it properly. As the account gets older, it falls out of the "new" credit category, and you can expect your score to rise again.

If you open multiple new credit accounts (or attempt to), this can impact your score even further. This raises red flags for the credit bureaus that you might be overextended financially, and looking for ways to cover expenses. If this isn't the case, there's nothing you can do if you've already applied for multiple credit cards, lines of credit, or loans.

If you want to open a new account, do your research ahead of time and only apply for something you feel confident you'll be approved for. This is why pre-approvals are useful—so you don't apply for accounts you have no hope of qualifying for.

Variety

Credit bureaus also love to see that you have experience managing different types of credit—both loans and what's called revolving credit. Revolving credit simply refers to a credit card or line of credit that you can fill up and pay back down over and over.

Since loans like a mortgage or car loan have a declining balance, you simply want to show that you're paying the monthly payments on time. For revolving credit, the goal is to use your credit AND pay it down, without letting the balance get too high.

Ultimately, variety is something that comes with time, since you don't want to open too many accounts at once. If you're looking for a good place to start, especially if you have no credit history, a secured credit card can help you build credit. They're easy to get approved for because you secure the credit line with your own funds. If you can build a credit history with this over a year, you can improve your score and move on to another type of credit: maybe a car, or another credit card.

How to Build Credit if You Don't Have It

Typically, the people who don't have any credit history are newly minted adults. However, it's possible to start building credit even before you turn 18, however it can require parental help. If you're a parent, maybe you want to give your teenagers a head start with their credit, so they have more opportunities after they turn 18. Regardless, let's discuss some strategies to kickstart that credit history.

Co-Signing Loans

One of the best ways to start building credit history, or get a boost on an application for new credit, is to have a cosigner. For example, if your credit score is low (or non-existent), it would be difficult to qualify for a car loan on your own. If, however, you can have a family member co-sign on the loan, you get the strength of their credit score on your application.

When you co-sign a loan, you're saying that you'll be responsible for payments, however that doesn't mean you have to make the payments. If you're co-signing on a car loan for your teenager, you'll likely come to an agreement that they make the monthly payments. However, if they can't, you'll be the backup, and your credit score is on the line. In other words, be sure your teenager knows the responsibility of the loan.

However, in a successful arrangement, both of your credit scores will benefit from the consistent, on-time payments of the loan.

Secured Credit Cards

A secured credit card is simply a credit card that is backed by a physical dollar amount, oftentimes one of your choosing. For example, you could apply for a secured card with $500 as collateral, and your credit limit would then be $500.

The credit card would act just like any other credit card, with the added benefit of having collateral to draw from if you default (although you DON'T want to default). These are good for people who are building their credit, even with no credit history, because they're easy to qualify for. And since the credit limit is relatively low, it's good practice for someone who doesn't have experience managing a credit card.

It's also possible to open low-balance store cards with little to no credit history. These can have high interest rates, however, so be aware when applying. And avoid getting a store card at a store that's too tempting if you like to shop!

Authorized Users

Adding someone to your credit card as an authorized user is

another way to help them build credit. Generally, parents can add their children as authorized users, or spouses can add each other. This would allow the other person to have their own credit card attached to the same line of credit. While they can make purchases, they can also benefit from the card's history and on-time payments.

Essentially, all the goodness (or lack thereof) that comes from that particular card will also apply to the authorized users. However, the reverse is true—if you add an authorized user and they rack up a bunch of debt on that account, you'll both feel the sting.

If you're a parent and you're unsure whether you want to give your child access to your credit lines, yet you still want to help them build credit, you can add them as an authorized user to your account and simply keep it to yourself. That way they can't add to the bill. Just note that your actions will still affect their credit history, so be sure you're setting them up for success.

How to Improve Your Existing Credit History

If you already have credit history and you're less than satisfied with your results, don't worry just yet. There is still plenty you can do to improve your score. It just takes patience and commitment.

Make Payments on Time

One of the best things you can do on an ongoing basis to improve your credit score is to keep making payments, and make them on-time. It's okay if it's just the minimum balance, which is much better than not paying at all.

Reduce Your Credit Usage

Next, you want to think about how much revolving credit you're using. As mentioned earlier, you generally want to use less than

50% of your total credit limit.

Let's say you have three credit cards: one with a $2,000 limit, one with a $500 limit, and one with a $750 limit. Total, your revolving credit is $3,250. This means that you want to keep your total usage across the cards under $1,625. It doesn't matter if it's all on one card, or spread across three, as long as your overall usage is under the 50% mark.

Do NOT Cancel Your Cards

Sometimes, when people pay off a credit card that they've been struggling with, they're tempted to cancel it. However, this does a few things that can negatively impact your overall score.

First, if that credit card was your oldest credit card and you cancel it, your score can drop. This goes back to the credit history—credit bureaus want to see how long you've been working at your score. By closing your oldest account, you're effectively wiping away part of your history. It reflects well on your score to have an older account, even if there's no balance.

Additionally, by closing the account, you reduce your overall available credit. So let's go back to the three credit cards example above. If you paid off the $750 credit card and then you close it, you're reducing your total revolving credit to $2,500. Now, you want to keep your balance below $1,250. On the flip side, if you leave the account open and don't put anything else on it, you can get your credit usage well below 50%, which is even better for your credit score.

If you're afraid that you're going to use the credit card if you don't cancel it, consider freezing it instead. That way you can't use it, and you'll still get the benefits of the history and the available credit.

Do a Balance Transfer

If one of your objectives, in addition to credit repair, is debt repayment, sometimes a balance transfer can help. However, a balance transfer requires opening a new account, so be aware that it might hurt your credit score before it helps it.

That being said, there are many credit cards that have 12-18 month welcome offers that provide a 0% interest rate on balance transfers. If you have a credit card with a high credit limit and you're confident that you can pay it off over the course of the welcome offer, this can be a great way to save on interest cost.

In turn, this can boost your credit score because you'll have more available credit, which reduces your credit usage percentage. And if you're committed to paying off the balance in 12 -18 months, your score will benefit from that, too.

Just be careful and read the fine print—sometimes on 0% interest offers, you may have to pay back interest if you don't reduce the balance to zero within the offer period. This differs from card to card, just be sure you know what you're signing up for.

Increase Your Credit Limits

Another quick way to boost your credit score is, once again, to decrease your credit usage. And the fastest way to do that, aside from paying off your credit cards (which, of course, you should still do), is to get a line of credit increase. Some cards will do this automatically for you over time, as you prove yourself to make on-time payments. However, it's also possible to request credit increases, too. After all, if you're going to keep your cards for a long time, you want them to grow with you. It doesn't make sense to have a $500 credit limit forever.

By increasing your credit limit, you effectively decrease the percentage of your credit usage, which boosts your score. You also increase the overall amount of credit you have access to, which can increase your score.

What you don't necessarily want to do is open a new credit card. This can have the same effect, however, you'll get dinged for that "new account." While this will fall away eventually, you want to be mindful of what objectives you're working toward. If you're improving your score to buy a house, you don't want to have a bunch of new accounts pop up.

Additionally, don't increase your credit limit just to spend it!

PART 4: WHAT WEALTHY FAMILIES DO

WHILE BUDGETING MAY AT FIRST seem like a concern only for a certain income level, I often see wealthy families caught in the cycle of personal finance mistakes, too. While the motivations and outcomes may differ, the truth is that even those with great wealth can make money mistakes that cost them. Here's what I see:

Mistake 1: Avoiding Money Conversations

If you have money, you should be having conversations about your money with your loved ones. No one is exempt from this, and yet one of the biggest mistakes I see, particularly in wealthy families, is a lack of conversation about money matters.

Here are just a few reasons people may avoid talking about money with their parents, spouse, children, and so on.

- **Fear of judgment.** We all fear being judged, to some degree. And many people attach a sense of personal worth to their financial situation. Whether people see them as too successful, not successful enough, or somewhere in between, they may link these judgments to their intelligence, decision-making skills, and other attributes.

- **Discomfort.** Regardless of whether there is judgment being passed, it can be uncomfortable to talk about money due to feelings of insecurity, shame, or guilt. Especially if someone "should" know better.
- **Lack of knowledge.** Some people may not know how to talk about money in a productive way. They may not know how to ask for help or how to share their financial information with others safely, so they don't do it at all.
- **Cultural taboo.** In some cultures, talking about money is considered taboo. This may be because money is seen as a private matter or because it is associated with greed or materialism.

Whatever the reason, avoiding money conversations can have negative consequences. It can lead to financial problems, strained relationships, and missed opportunities. And if you aren't having money conversations with your children, you're not helping them to inherit your wealth responsibly.

If you are afraid of talking about money, there are things you can do to overcome your fear. Here are a few tips:

- **Start small.** Don't try to have one big money conversation all at once. Start by talking about small things, such as your spending habits or your best (or your worst) investment.
- **Find a trusted friend or family member.** Talk to someone you trust about your financial situation. Opening up to a loved one, especially one who is not directly involved with your finances, can help you get your bearings for more personal money conversations.
- **Seek professional help.** If you are struggling to talk about money, consider seeking professional help from a financial therapist.

Talking about money can be difficult, but it is important to have these conversations. By opening up about your financial situation, you can build stronger relationships, make better financial decisions, and achieve your financial goals. This has the added benefit of helping you to raise financially competent children for the next generation.

Mistake 2: Spending all of your income.

Many wealthy families fall into the trap of thinking that they can afford to spend all their investment income and/or earned income. This can lead to financial problems down the road because inflation and technological change tend to run expenses up much higher than expected. Additionally, without an emergency/opportunity fund, you're unprepared for the unexpected twists and turns of life. Remember cash flow issues don't go away, they just get bigger zero's on them.

The solution, however, isn't to budget and categorize your spending. Instead, you've got to save first (and budget never). This means setting aside money for savings before you even start spending. While it may seem counterintuitive, putting aside your savings BEFORE you spend your money is actually the best way to stay on track with your finances and enjoy your income at the same time. Not to mention, you'll be preparing yourself for the future.

There are several reasons why saving first is better than budgeting at all. First, it helps you to focus on your long-term goals. When you budget, you are essentially making a plan for how you will spend your money in the coming month. While this can help you track your expenses and curb overspending, it's a short-term mindset. It doesn't require any forethought, and as such, budgeting often falls short of people's expectations in the long run, especially when making spending decisions based on what you have left over after you have paid your bills, rather than on what is important to you in the long run.

Second, saving first helps you to build your financial discipline, which is necessary even in wealthy families. When you have to make a conscious decision to save money before you spend any, it forces you to think about your priorities. This can help you to develop the discipline that you need to stick to your financial goals.

If you are a wealthy family, I urge you to instill a "save first, budget never" mentality in your children, too. This is the best way to ensure that they have a strong financial foundation for the future.

Here are some tips for teaching your children about saving first:

- **Talk about the importance of saving money.** Explain that saving money is a way for them to reach their goals, like buying a bike or a car. Help them to set age-appropriate financial goals. This could be something as simple as saving 20 percent of their earnings (via chores, a job, or an entrepreneurial pursuit). We recommend the app + account called DinnerTable for kids and Currence for adults.

- **Make saving money a habit.** Create a structure where you can automate transfers directly to their savings accounts, so they're more likely to keep it there. If they get cash, help them to split it into categories such as spending and saving money, maybe even a donate or invest category. We don't recommend allowances which tend to create an entitlement attitude.

- **Reward your children for saving money.** This could be something simple like providing them an annual bonus, or paying them a small interest rate on top of the bank's interest rate. For example, you could give them a five or ten cent bonus for every dollar they save.

By teaching your children about saving first, you are giving them the gift of financial freedom.

A Story of Two Sisters

Once upon a time, there were two friends named Alice and Beatrice.

Alice's parents taught her to save first, and budget never. They set up an automatic transfer from her checking account to her savings account every month, and they rewarded her for saving money. As a result, Alice had a large savings account by the time she graduated high school, and she carried that knowledge with her to college.

Beatrice's parents did not teach her about saving money. They told her to focus on her education and her career, and they said that she would have plenty of time to worry about money later. As a result, Beatrice had very little savings when she graduated from high school, and college didn't leave much room for her to worry about saving.

After college, Alice and Beatrice were both happy to accept positions in careers they enjoyed. They moved to the same city, happy to be in each other's orbit. However, Alice's ample savings made it possible for her to put a down payment on a house, and even make a few investments. Meanwhile, Beatrice could only rent an apartment, since she didn't have much saved.

Over the course of a few years, both Alice and Beatrice found themselves married and with children. But while Beatrice and her spouse had to keep working to support their new baby, Alice was able to take a longer maternity leave and enjoy time at home. Her savings provided an ample cushion to do so, stress-free.

Over the years, Alice and her spouse found that their financial position only improved. They had good communication, and Alice was even able to share many of her good habits with her family. She was able to convert her term life insurance into whole life insurance so that it was an asset rather than an expense, and one that could provide for her family in an emergency, too. Over time, Alice adopted the Currence app+account structure to automate her save-first habit, and she helped her kids use the DinnerTable app to learn more about saving, too.

Beatrice, on the other hand, struggled financially. She and her spouse had to work long hours to make ends meet, and they never felt financially free. Beatrice was embarrassed about her lack of money knowledge so she never spoke to her spouse about it, nor her children, which only perpetuated the problem that her own parents passed on to her. She didn't even speak to Alice about her troubles, because she was afraid of judgment.

The two women remained friends over the course of their lives, yet if they had only communicated about money, who knows how Beatrice might have grown. Instead, the topic felt too taboo, so they kept their friendship to other topics.

The story of Alice and Beatrice is one that is all too common in today's world. And it just goes to show that saving first is even better than budgeting, because it gave Alice a lot of options and opportunities on her journey. Beatrice's budget, on the other hand, only kept her head above the water. When you save first, you are building a financial foundation that will support you in the long run. When you budget, it can feel impossible to "get ahead."

If you want to be financially successful, start saving first today.

A Very Special Resource

I've been honored throughout the years of helping families with their finances to watch a few wealthy families and how they handle money and budgeting in particular. I can say with 100% confidence that what I heard Scott Donnell say when I met him was spot on: Wealthy families save first. AND they also pay attention to the details of how cash flows through their lives.

For many people, especially young adults heading out on their own, it IS necessary to "budget," especially if you define budget as a "spending guideline." With that in mind, we are so grateful to have gotten the permission to reprint the Value Creation Kid guide on the following pages. We encourage you to buy the full book—*Value Creation Kid*—for everyone in your inner circle.

Value Creation Kid
Resource Guide

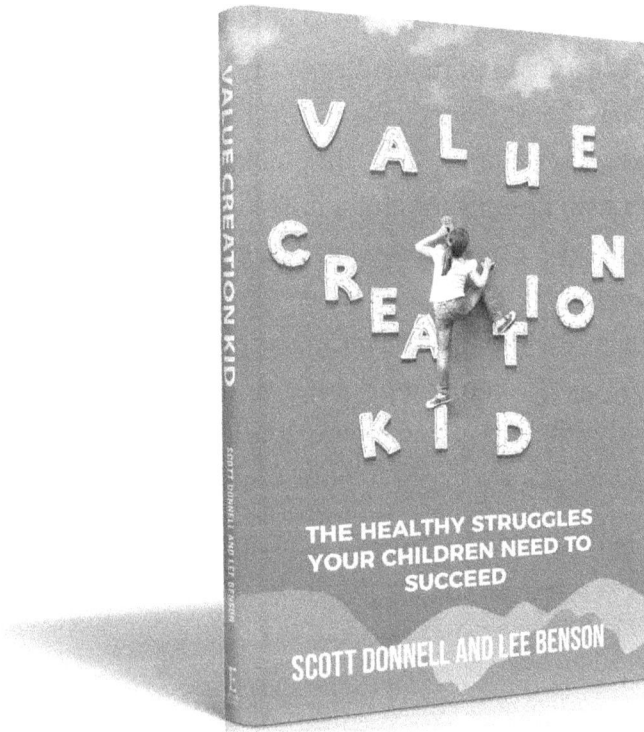

90 Healthy Struggles

Relationships
- Family Culture: What does it mean to have your last name; building a family brand.
- Create Your Mission, Vision, and Values for your family, friends, and future.
- Reputation: how to build a good reputation and why you cannot afford to lose it.
- Friendship: how to be a good friend.
- Finding a Good Mentor
- The 4 Rules to Credibility defined by Dan Sullivan, co-founder of Strategic Coach® : show up on time, do what you say, finish what you start, say please and thank you.

Communication
- Negotiation: How to compromise, create win-wins, techniques, listening
- Persuasion: The art of persuasion, techniques, psychology, tips, why it's important
- Public Speaking: Tips, techniques, and practicing in front of family and friends
- Body Language: What it means, how to have good body language
- Making Conversation: Small talk, being interested, asking good questions
- How to Forgive and Apologize

Mindset
- Positive Attitude and Constant Improvement
- Abundance Thinking vs. Scarcity Thinking
- Leadership Mentality: How to take more and more ownership of your life
- Goal Setting and Momentum
- Problem-Solving: "We cannot solve our problems with the same thinking we used to create them." —Einstein
- Time Management: Scheduling calendar appointments (dentist/doctor/nails for mom), busyness, chunking your time, etc.
- Teamwork and Collaboration: Adopting a "Who Not How" way of thinking
- Avoiding FOMO (Fear of Missing Out) Traps
- Habits of Success: Be proactive, set goals, prioritize, solve problems, create value, listen, think win-win, and keep sharpening yourself
- Brain Hacks: Tips for memory, speed reading, remembering names, study hacks

Career Prep
- How to Get a Job: Preparing for a job interview, research, presentation, questions to ask
- Building a Resume
- How to Write a Cover Letter
- Letters of Recommendation
- Internships and Apprenticeships
- Writing Skills - Sales Copy vs. Educational Copy
- Preparing for College: ROI of college, education and career goals, budget and tuition planning, dorm rooms, rent, meal plan, laundry, banking, choosing a college, FAFSA, how to get grants and scholarships

Financial Competency
- Talking About Money at Home: Values, attitudes towards money, openness to discussion
- What is the Economy: Differences between various economic systems, movement of goods/services, supply and demand, chain of production, Gross Domestic Product, and creating value
- Time Value of Money
- Delayed Gratification vs. Instant Gratification and how to practice it at home
- Debits vs. Credits
- Compounding Interest
- Earning
- Saving
- Spending
- Sharing
- Investing
- Protecting
- Borrowing
- Taxes and Insurance

Technology
- Social Media: Healthy vs. Unhealthy
- Online Security and safety against harm
- Personal Data and how your data is used and sold

Career Skills
- Selling Yourself, Selling Ideas, Selling to Others
- Marketing: Content creation, writing, hooks, sales copy, digital marketing, e-commerce
- Engineering: Aerospace, Agricultural, Architectural, Automotive, Biological, Chemical, Civil, Computer, Electrical, Environmental, Geological, Geotechnical, Industrial, Manufacturing, Marine, Mechanical, Mining, Nuclear, Petroleum, Structural, Systems
- Event Planning: Put on an event for 50 people, do a Children's Business Fair
- Nonprofits: How they are funded, how they help the world, mission work, services, research
- Creating a Business LLC
- Financial Planning
- Law and Contracts
- Health and Fitness
- Science and Medicine
- Artificial Intelligence
- Machine Learning
- Software Development
- Digital and Creative Design
- Basic Construction

Budgeting and Planning
- Travel Planning: Plan the next family trip
- Finding your way home from anywhere and how to use a map
- Shopping 101: All the tips for buying food at the store
- Consumerism (Consumer Awareness/Buying Power)
- Setting a Monthly Budget: Reviewing Bank Statements, Balancing a Checkbook

Investing
- Credit Score
- Financial Planning
- Insurance
- Risk Management
- Blockchain Technology
- Venture Capital
- Trading
- Real Estate

Practical Skills
- Physical Fitness and Training
- Nutrition: learning what protein, carbohydrates, and fats do for your body
- Hygiene: Shaving, cleaning your room, showering, brushing teeth, and body odor
- Manners: Tie a tie, etiquette, chivalry, shaking hands, opening doors, making introductions
- Pet Care: Grooming, feeding, cleaning up after, washing, walking, training
- First Aid Basics: How to handle a cold, the flu, cuts and scrapes, calling 911, what if you see someone unconscious or sibling choking, things to watch out for
- Knot tying: How to tie ten of the most popular knots
- Laundry: Washing, folding, what not to wash, stains, and sewing skills
- Home Improvement: Air filters, turning off water, basic plumbing and electrical, unclogging a toilet, painting a wall, changing a lightbulb, proper closet organization
- Navigating the Kitchen: Basic cooking, using a stove and oven, meal prep, deep cleaning, tiny habits in the kitchen
- Car Maintenance: buying a car, changing a tire, or oil, or filters, jumpstarting a car
- Survival Skills and Preparation
- Outdoor skills: Farming, cleaning a fish, hiking, camping, hunting, caring for the environment
- Voting, Democracy, and Government: why they matter and what is civic duty

To start your path to financial literacy, head over to: ProsperityParents.com

Gigs List

Home Gigs

💪 Action

Sweep the floors
Vacuum the house (ages 12+)
Pick up toys (ages <12)
Take out trash and recycling
Clean up common areas
Organize a closet
Wash and fold laundry
Clean the windows
Organize a bookshelf
Clean and vacuum your room
Assemble furniture (ages 12+)
Clean entire kitchen
Clean inside of trash cans
Mop floor
Wash/Put Away the dishes
Wipe off counters and sink
Unload/put away groceries
Clean inside of fridge
Make family breakfast
Make lunches for school
Make family dinner
Clean entire bathroom
Sweep the floors
Vacuum the house (ages 12+)

Pick up toys (ages <12)
Take out trash and recycling
Clean up common areas
Organize a closet
Wash and fold laundry
Clean the windows
Organize a bookshelf
Clean and vacuum your room
Assemble furniture (ages 12+)
Clean entire kitchen
Clean inside of trash cans
Mop floor
Wash/Put Away the dishes
Wipe off counters and sink
Unload/put away groceries
Clean inside of fridge
Make family breakfast
Make lunches for school
Make family dinner
Clean entire bathroom
Pick up from school (ages 12+)
Babysit (ages 12+)
Help with homework - 30 min
Pack car for trip

🧠 Brain

Write/give a personal thank you card
Read non-fiction book
Communication
Music
Positive Self Esteem
Craftsmanship
Skip the sugar
Exercise
Journal
Take a break from TV
Setting Big Goals by Bejamin Hardy
Watch a true inspirational hero story
Read an inspirational biography
Write my future...
I value ...
My Passions are...
I am good at...
I can solve...

Community Gigs

Yard work
Babysit
Dog walking
Dog sitting
Gardening
Car washing
Unload groceries
Help moving
Yard sale help
Plant watering

House cleaning
Errand running
Leaf raking
Snow shoveling
Grocery shopping
Newspaper delivery
Delivering flyers
Painting fences
Home repairs
Cleaning gutters

Garage cleaning
Tutoring
Music / art lessons
Computer help
Unloading groceries
Garage cleaning
Tutoring
Music lessons
Art lessons

**To start your path
to financial literacy,
head over to:
ProsperityParents.com**

150 Business Ideas

- 3-D Printed Objects
- Apparel Company
- Aromatherapy Items
- Baby Items
- Bags - sewn, recycled, knitted, repurposed
- Baked Goods, non-perishable
- Barbie Clothes
- Bath Soaps / Bombs
- Birdhouses / Feeders
- Board Games
- Bookmarks
- Bottles of Lemonade
- Bracelets
- Bubble Bath
- Bubble Wands
- Bunting
- Buttons
- Camping Set
- Candles
- Candy Bouquets / Arrangements
- Candy Sushi
- Capes / Ponchos
- Caramel Corn / Snacks
- Cartoon Your Face
- Cell Phone Accessories
- Chalkboards
- Chew Toys
- Children's Book
- Chocolates
- Cleaning Aquariums
- Cleaning Litter Boxes
- Clocks
- Cloth Napkins
- Coasters
- Collecting Mail
- Coloring Books
- Comics / Comic Art
- Cookbook
- Cookie in a Can
- Cookie Mix in a Jar
- Craft Kits
- Creative Cards
- Decals
- Decorated/Painted Tins
- Decoupage Jars
- Dog Bones
- Doll Accessories

- Dry Cocoa in a Jar
- Duct Tape Wallet/Crafts
- Encouragement Jars
- Erasers/Pencil Toppers
- Face Masks
- Fairy Wings and Wands
- Felted Wool Crafts
- Finger Knit projects
- Fitness classes
- Fleece Blankets
- Friendship Bracelets
- Hair Bows
- Hair Extensions
- Hair Ties / Head Bands
- Hand Sanitizer
- Handbags for groceries
- Handmade Stuffed Animals
- Hats / Caps
- Holiday Ornaments / Decorations
- Home Décor
- Homemade Bowls
- Homemade Wrapping Paper
- Honey Products
- Ink Tiles & Ornaments
- Jams /Jellies
- Jewelry
- Keychains
- Kits - DIY Crafts, Science Experiments, Food, Movie Night
- Knitting Scarves & Hats
- Leather Key rings / Wallets
- Linen Sprays
- Lotions
- Magic Tricks
- Magnets
- Managing Social Media
- Marshmallow Shooters
- Metal crafts
- Movies
- Name Holders
- Oils
- Olives
- Online Research
- Origami Paper
- Airplanes
- Original Poems

- Ornaments
- Painted Artwork
- Painted Rocks
- Paperweights
- Painted Skateboards
- Paper Mache Crafts
- Para Cord Bracelets
- Keychains
- Party Decorations
- Party Helper
- Pen/Pencil Holders
- Perfume
- Personalized Pet Dishes
- Pet Collars
- Photo Cards
- Pickles
- Picture Blankets
- Piggy Banks
- Pillowcases
- Pillows – throw, holiday
- Placemats
- Plant Hangers
- Plants
- Plaster Crafts
- Polymer Clay Figures
- Polymer Clay Jewelry
- Poop Scooping for Dogs
- Pottery Plates / Bowls
- Purses
- Puzzles
- PVC Pipe Toys
- Rainbow Loom Crafts
- Rubber band Jewelry
- Scrapbooks / Memory Books
- Seashell Crafts
- Seeds / Seedlings
- Sew Headbands
- Sew Zipper Pouches
- Shoes
- Signs
- Slime
- Sling Shots
- Smartphone Stand
- Snacks / Munchies
- Social Media Management
- Socks with Faces
- Songs
- Spices

- Sports/Pokémon Cards
- Stained Glass
- Stick Puppets
- Stickers
- Stress Balls
- Sugar Scrubs
- Survival Kits
- Teaching Computer Courses
- Terrariums
- Tie Dye Shirts / Bandanas / Hats / Shoelaces
- Tissue Paper Crafts
- Toy Baskets
- T-Shirts
- Tutoring / Life Advice
- Used Books
- Walking Dogs
- Walking Sticks
- Wall Art
- Water Bottles
- Wax Art
- Websites – Create & Update
- Web Videos
- Wine Glass Charms
- Woodworking
- Yarn Crafts
- Zipper Pulls

To start your path to financial literacy, head over to: ProsperityParents.com

The 3 E's

Expectations: Clarifying what you expect your kids to do in the home without pay

Expenses: Listing the expenses that your kids are now in charge of paying for

Extra Pay: Creating Home Gigs, a list of ways that your kids can earn extra money at home to cover their spending list.

E expectations   **E** expenses   **E** extra pay

THE VALUE
CREATION CYCLE™

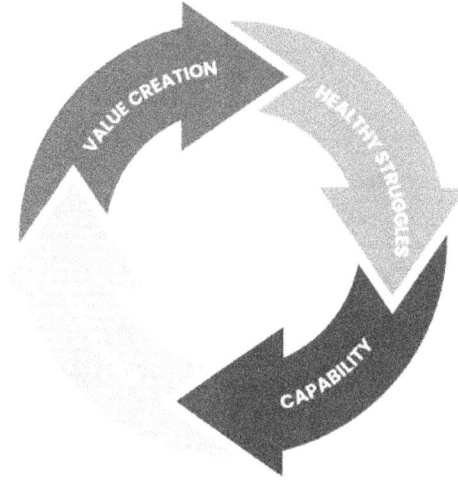

VALUE CREATION

HEALTHY STRUGGLES

CAPABILITY

VALUE CREATION
KID MATRIX™

Anxious Self-Doubter	Value Creation Kid™
Lazy Victim	Entitled Taker

CAPABLE

CONFIDENT

About the Authors

Kim D. H. Butler is helping Americans build wealth... first in their minds, with specific thinking methods, secondly on their balance sheets with life insurance cash value that grows with guarantees and finally with an income for life product that enables more guarantees and prosperous mindsets. Kim is President of Prosperity Thinkers, a money methods firm that serves clients in all 50 states. Along with her husband Todd Langford of Truth Concepts financial software, Kim is also the co-founder of the Prosperity Economics Movement.

A recognized expert on whole life insurance and financial strategies. Kim has authored paradigm-shifting books such as: *Live Your Life Insurance*, *Busting the Life Insurance Lies*, and *Perpetual Wealth*. She has been handling money since 4th grade when her parents gave her a milk cow. After college, she joined a bank and then a life insurance agency combined with a money management company.

Driven to find a better way, Kim studied the commonalities between wealth builders. She observed what worked and didn't work in the real world, and found synergy between certain strategies and principles. These common principles later became the 7 Principles of Prosperity so widely used.

In 1999, Kim dedicated herself to these principles of Prosperity Economics. Her work has been recommended by financial thought leaders and authors such as Robert Kiyosaki (*Rich Dad, Poor Dad*), Tom Dyson, publisher of the *Palm Beach Letter* investment newsletter, Tom Wheelright (*Tax-Free Wealth*), and Garrett Gunderson (*Killing Sacred Cows*). She enjoys writing books (as long as she has help!) and podcasting at The Prosperity Podcast on iTunes.

You can reach Kim through ProsperityThinkers.com.

E.P. Hagenlocher is a writer and personal finance enthusiast from southern Illinois. After graduating college, she was led to work with Kim Butler on some writing projects, and the rest is history. Now she enjoys writing about financial concepts that can help people transform their lives for the better. Through this work, she hopes to make financial principles easy to understand and implement, so that financial freedom feels accessible to anyone.

About the Prosperity Economics Movement

Before the rise of qualified retirement plans, the ever-present 401(k), and the financial planning industry, people built wealth with diligence and common-sense strategies. Investors created wealth through building equity and ownership in properties, businesses, and participating (dividend-paying) whole life insurance. Only a few dabbled in Wall Street stocks or built "portfolios" on paper.

Wealthy people, in fact, have never stopped practicing what we call "Prosperity Economics."

Today, the common investor is steered away from traditional wealth-building methods. Instead, they are confronted with a confusing labyrinth of funds, rates, and complex financial instruments of questionable value. Mutual funds have become so complicated that even the people who sell them can't often explain them well, nor predict when investors are about to lose money. Worse yet, over time, over 30 percent of the average investor's wealth is drained away in fees to a financial industry rife with conflicts of interest.

The Prosperity Economics Movement (PEM) is a rediscovery of the traditional, simple, and trusted ways to grow and protect your money. It was founded in order to provide American investors an alternative to "typical" financial planning, showing us how to control our own wealth instead of delegating our financial futures to corporations and the government.

In Prosperity Economics, wealth isn't measured by how much money you have, but by how much freedom you have with your money. The focus is on cash flow rather than net worth. Liquidity, control, and safety are valued over uncertain hopes of a high rate of return.

Typical financial planning is better than nothing and will get you partway up the hill. Yet we want to show you an even better way: the top of the Prosperity mountain. Prosperity Economics shows you how to grow your wealth safely and reliably, with optimal financial flexibility and cash flow.

While Prosperity Economics Strategies and thinking have been around for many years, they were only recently coined under that term and organized as a movement by financial author Kim Butler and financial software developer Todd Langford.

The Prosperity Economics Movement is a not-for-profit organization comprising financial experts who practice Prosperity Economics and individuals who would like to learn how to apply the principles of Prosperity Economics to improve their lives. This book is part of a growing body of information that supports the organization and its members.

To learn more, visit ProsperityEconomics.org.

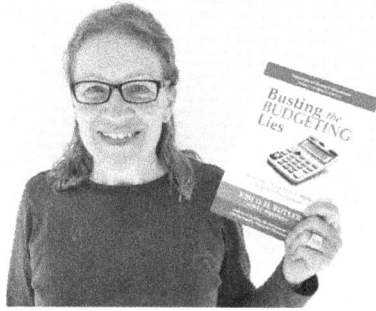

Additionally, as our gift to you, the QR code will
provide you an additional white paper focused on
Income Strategies at
ProsperityEconomics.org/permission

www.ingramcontent.com/pod-product-compliance
Lightning Source LLC
Chambersburg PA
CBHW050513210326
41521CB00011B/2437